TERMITE REPAIR

George Demaree

Copyright U.S.A.

Published by Tradesman
P. O. Box 7654
San Jose, California 95150

ISBN 0-935831-00-2

INDEX

CHAPTER 1

TERMITE INSPECTION

In this book I will try to explain and show in diagrams the easiest and the best way I have found to do repairs. (There always seems to be a better way to do just about everything, finding that better way is a lifetime search.)

I worked for years in the termite repair business, first as a repairman, then as an inspector and later owning my own company.

Termite and fungus repair in some ways is like surgery, whereas you have to locate the problem and remove or repair only that part which is infected. It has been said to be like a cancer, and it will only get worse as time goes on, if not corrected. Some houses I have seen have so much damage, the cost to have a termite company come in and make repairs, dollars wise, it would seem to be cheaper to rebuild.

First and most important the

structure should be inspected by a competent termite inspector. Builders and contractors are not usually qualified. The inspector will write out a report stating what he has found and recommendations for corrections. After you receive the termite report, you will know where you stand as far as termite infestation or damage are concerned. This termite report should also include items which may lead to infestation or damage.

The termite inspectors in most states are licensed by the state, through lengthy written examinations, and are closely regulated. In most states all termite reports must be sent to a state agency where each one is checked for errors. Most states also have state inspectors which re-inspect any structure in question. When two termite inspections are made about the same time and the same conditions are not reported, you know you can expect the state to check, so have the structure checked by a termite company. Sometimes there is a fee for the inspection, but it's money well spent. (Some companies inspect for free.)

I was a carpenter for 10 years before going into the termite work. More than once, we carpenters were told to build with wood that was full of termites.

It was a common practice to let cellulose debris fall under the subflooring during construction. However, I, and I am sure the foreman on the construction job, did not realize the problem we were causing. So, have the structure inspected by a termite company.

WARNING

THE AUTHOR OR THE PUBLISHER CANNOT ASSUME RESPONSIBILITY REGARDING THE USE OF TOOLS, CHEMICALS, OR THE MANNER OF REPAIRS.

PROTECT THE PUBLIC BY KEEPING

THEM AWAY FROM WORK AREA

WATCH YOUR HEAD FOR LOW OBJECTS

CHECK BEFORE YOU CUT, THERE MAY

BE HIDDEN DANGERS, LIKE PIPES OR

ELECTRIC WIRES

CHAPTER 2

CELLULOSE DEBRIS

Cellulose debris is any wood, paper, cardboard, wood shaving, rags, books or anything that is made of cellulose. This may include stumps and roots from trees that were cut down when the house was built, also form boards and stakes that were not removed at the time of construction.

The reason to remove the cellulose debris (CD) from the soil under the house or apartments is that it is food for the insect, mainly the subterranean termite, but also old house borer, beetles, other termites and fungus (wood rot). These infections and infestations can attack the wood structure of the building.

The general rule is to remove all cellulose debris of a size that can be raked. I find the best way for me, is to use a cardboard box and push it ahead of me as I crawl around the subarea picking up cellulose debris.

If there should be roots, stumps,

form boards or stakes that are (impractical) to be removed, it is sometimes permissible to remove what is practical and chemically treat the remainder with a fungicide.

I like to use copper green fungicide because if and when the subarea is inspected again, the one doing the inspection can see that these areas have been chemically treated. (See Diagram A-1)

Old tree stumps that are not completely removed also should be chemically treated with copper green and covered with plastic. Place rocks or bricks on plastic to keep in place. (See A-5)

Wood blocks under pipes should be removed and bricks put in their place or the pipes should be tied up to the wood members by a metal plumber strap. (See Diagram A-2)

Sometimes there will be wood blocks under heat ducts. These wood blocks should be replaced with masonry or tied to the structure by wire. These heat ducts are light in weight and can be easily supported. You might check for damage to the heat ducts. Termite inspectors, plumbers, telephone men and others that have to work in the subarea, have a hard time getting past the heat ducts and sometimes the heat ducts are damaged. (See A-3)

At times, there will be other appliances in the subarea, heat pump units and other things, (if they) are set on wood blocks (A-4) they should also be replaced with masonry.

Some of the wood scrap (CD) you remove will have a "checked" area. This is fungus or wood rot. (See A-6). The fungi is spread from scrap wood to wood members in the subarea by microscopic spores. If you see what looks like a toadstool or mushroom, (remove this also), as this is the fungi seed pod. Then chemically treat the area with copper green to kill the seed spores. These chemical fungicides can be purchased at hardware and building supply stores. All chemicals should be used in accordance with manufacturer's instructions and in a safe manner.

I recommend the use of protective hand and eye wear. Gloves are most important, as these chemicals stain everything. The smell is strong also, but when dry there is little or no smell.

Whenever I go into the subarea of a structure, I always wear coveralls, a pair of kneepads, work shoes and gloves. When I am going to remove cellulose debris from subarea, I will have a cardboard box with a flashlight, a hammer and a screwdriver. (See Tools)

When coming out of the subarea and

into the home, I remove the coveralls, kneepads, and gloves to keep the dirt out of the house, and save myself the job of cleaning the area. Sometimes I spread newspapers at the access hole, especially if the area around the access is carpeted.

If the access to the subarea is on the outside of the building, the job is a great deal easier. All you have to be careful of, when working from the outside, is the plants and the family dog.

While under the structure it is a good time to check and repair any foundation vents that have the screening broken. A new piece of screening can be bent to fit over the existing screen, and nailed to the wood members. This is important to keep cats, rats and other animals out of the subarea. Many of these animals enter the open subarea (including birds) and not finding their way out, die.

This is not a good place for the family pet either, especially if the soil has been chemically treated. The pet will get the dried chemical on its feet and then lick the chemical off. This chemical can be very harmful to any animal or human, so wash with soap and water after working in the subarea.

CHAPTER 3

EXCESSIVE MOISTURE

Excessive moisture in the soil is a reason for concern, as the moisture evaporates and condenses on the structural wood members and causes wood rot and fungus to grow.

E. M., which is the usual symbol found on termite reports, indicates excessive moisture conditions. On some termite reports this will be a local area, and on other reports it will be the entire subarea.

In many cases the excessive moisture conditions is caused by over watering. When water enters the subarea, by way of the foundation vents, this is easy to correct. With care, to protect the foundation vents from the sprinklers.

Sometimes the soil becomes saturated with water from rain or over watering.

The soil below the house is lower than the outside soil, therefore seep-page will occur. Water always seeks the lowest level, which in this case happens to be the subarea (under the structure).

The rain is usually temporary and will stop and let the soil dry and the over watering can be corrected. Sometimes, however, the water table is high in the area in which your building is built, or there is a run-off from the higher land area around your property, allowing moisture to seep to the level of your subarea. In this case drainage must be provided, such as drain tile (which is pipe with holes in the top of the pipe which collects the moisture and diverts it to another area). There are also sump pumps, which when installed in a pit (below the subarea) pumps out moisture which collects in the pit. (See Diagrams F-7 and F-8)

If the excessive moisture is not too bad, then it can probably be removed with the addition of more foundation vents. In some cases just the removal of shrubbery allows good cross ventilation. Many times grass is found blocking foundation vents, also storage in alleyways on the side of the house or apartment.

At times the structure is built in such a way that additional vents are not practical and the moisture is not too excessive, then as a secondary measure, plastic can be laid out over the subarea soil, thereby protecting the wood structure of the building. Check plastic from year to year.

It should be noted that in some geographic areas the temperature and the humidity are perfect for the growth of fungus (wood rot). Some of these areas are the Gulf Coast states of the United States, the Northwest Coast (Oregon, Washington state), and the South Atlantic states are also highly susceptible to fungus damage (wood rot).

Excessive moisture conditions can also be caused by gutters and down spouts that are not properly cleaned or repaired. They should be directed away from the structure, also the lot should be graded to divert water away from structure on all sides. Plumbing leaks can also cause wet soil conditions. (See Fungus Damage)

Planters that are not sealed so that they hold in the moisture are prime sites for excessive moisture and fungus (rot) to the adjacent areas in the structure. (See Diagrams C-6 and section on Planters)

Peeling or blistered paint may be a sign of excessive moisture. These areas should be checked for damage.

Fascia boards and eaves are prime locations for fungus (rot) as moisture can, at times, stay for long periods of time, trapped by leaves and lack of drainage.

This excessive moisture should be corrected and repairs made. (See Diagram B-1) Any damage should be cut out and the remaining wood members treated with a fungicide such as penta, or copper green, to retard fungus growth. Then rebuild the section as needed. (See Diagrams B-1 and B-3)

The area behind the down spout is seldom, if ever, checked or painted. Down spouts do rust through. This pours much water on the siding, be it wood or stucco. This is a prime area to maintain, as it can lead to much hidden damage.

CHAPTER 4

DISHWASHERS

Dishwasher leaks can damage the floor and floor covering. If the floor is concrete, all that needs to be repaired is the dishwasher leak and install a new floor covering. Sometimes this is covered by insurance. Generally, the owner pays to repair the leaking dishwasher and the insurance company pays for the damage caused by the leak. However, all insurance coverage is different, but it's good to check into your insurance coverage.

If the dishwasher is on a wood floor, then the damage can be light or heavy. Much depends on how long the dishwasher has been leaking. If the leak in the dishwasher is just a fill hose or drain hose and if the damage is just to the subfloor, then the repair work can be done from under the floor. (This saves removing the dishwasher.) If covered by insurance, and if the dishwasher repairman will make two trips to remove (let you make repairs), and then replace the dishwasher. It would be a lot easier to make repairs from the top of the floor. (See F-3, F-4, F-5, F-9, F-10) However, if the damage is in front of the dishwasher and a new floor covering is going to be needed, the dishwasher will have to be removed, so repairs can be made. In this case, it is easier to cut out the damage as it shows itself. Start where the floor covering is bulged, or where damage is evident. Remove only the underlayment (which is particle board or plywood, probably 1/2" thick). Cut this out with a portable circular saw, set for 1/2" deep. If the damage goes into the subfloor, you will have to remove that also. After the subfloor is cut, so you have a hole, then you can see if other structural wood members are damaged. The termite report will probably explain how far the fungus (rot) damage has progressed and what parts of the structure are damaged. All wood parts of the structure, that have any damage or stains in this area, should be replaced and heavy treatment of fungicide is recommended. As I stated before, copper green is very good and building inspectors seem to like it best. Building inspectors should be notified each time you intend to do some type of structural repair. When you get your building permit, the office will more than likely inform you of the regulations. Diagrams F-2 and F-3 are drawings of subfloor, supporting wood members. And F-3 is bracing of the hole so new subfloor can be replaced. When nailing the bracing to the subfloor as shown in F-3, angle the nails to give more holding power. You don't want the brace to come loose when nailing on the last piece. Some structures will have joists under the subfloor. In this case, cut subfloor at the joist center, or cut subflooring on the side of joist closest to hole, and nail a piece of new wood to the joist to hold subfloor. If joist is damaged, cut out damaged part and replace with new. Nail with large nails (#16p or bigger). Paint or spray area with copper green or some other fungicide. (See Diagrams F-4, F-5, F-9, F10)

USE RUBBER GLOVES WHEN WORKING WITH
CEMENT, AS THE CHEMICALS IN THE
CEMENT CAN BURN THE SKIN

CLEAN WORK AREA

WASH BEFORE EATING

CHAPTER 5

WATER HEATERS

Hot water heaters that leak and damage the structure can show more damage because they leak day and night. The warm water is ideal for the growth of fungi (wood rot). These areas should be repaired and supported with extra bracing, as this area must support a great deal of weight.

To remove the water heater it is best to drain the water out of the water heater, using a garden hose attached to the bottom drain valve. The water can be directed to the garden or to a drain or sink. You must shut off the intake valve to the hot water heater, or turn the water off where it enters the structure. Make the repair in the same manner as were used in Diagrams F-3, F-4, F-5, F-9, F-10. Chemically treat with fungicide. Don't forget to call the building inspector. Some water heaters are set on a wood platform in the garage area. These platforms should be kept in good repair, as they carry a lot of weight. (Water basically weighs 8 lbs

per gallon.) If you multiply 8 x 10
gallons, 8 x 20 gallons, 8 x 40 gallons, you can see the amount of weight
on an area of about 2 foot square.

I have seen metal trays under hot
water heaters to catch and drain off
any water which may leak. I don't
know if they were homemade or where
they came from, if purchased. See
Drawing F-6 for one type pan you can
make or have made. Be sure to direct
moisture outside of the structure if
using a pan. Subarea soil should stay
dry.

CHAPTER 6

WATER CLOSETS

Water closets (toilets) that are leaking will sometimes show a bulge in the floor covering. In this case the water closet must be removed to make repairs. If damage is only to the underlayment, the building inspector may not need to be informed. However, if the damage extends into the supporting structure, you should notify the building inspector before you cover up the repairs. When repairing the underlayment, care should be taken to make the flooring as smooth as possible. Use any of the floor repair fillers that are available at building supply stores.

There is no need to remove the old floor covering in most cases, as that is your smoothest floor surface. Where it is necessary to cut away some of the floor covering, fill in the space with floor filler (available at floor covering stores also).

If you decide to have the floor covering installed by a linoleum layer, he will probably fill the small cracks and nicks before installing the floor covering.

The same is true of repairs made to the area at the bathtub and around sinks.

Washing machines also leak and their repair is basically the same, unless the damage is into the wood structure, then see Diagrams F-3, F-4, F-5, F-9, F-10. Chemically treat with fungicide (copper green) and call the building inspector. Use a good tub and tile seal at areas where the linoleum and the tub meet. Also be sure to seal areas of shower doors and tub enclosures (see Mixes and Seals).

I recommend installing new bolts at the water closet. At the time of repair, if any extra nut is put on the bolt at the top of the plumbing flange, the bolt will stand straight and strong. Then the bolt will not fall when replacing water closet. Always use a new seal. Sometimes I have had to use two seals, one on top of the other, to get a seal. The water closet should compress the wax seal. If the water closet sets on the new seal and the floor, when you first set the water closet, and you don't have to force the water closet down to the floor, by sitting on it or something, you may not have a good seal and this can cause the water closet to leak on the floor again. Don't try to pull the water closet down with the bolts, as this may tend to break the base of the water closet. Be sure the fixture is all the way down and then tighten the bolts with care.

Many linoleum layers like to seal around the base of the water closet with latex caulking.

LIFT USING YOUR LEGS, NOT YOUR BACK

WEAR EYE PROTECTING

WORK SAFELY

MAKE MORE TRIPS FOR A HEAVY LOAD
OR USE WHEELS, SAVE YOUR BACK

CHAPTER 7

SUBTERRANEAN TERMITES

Subs, as they are referred to in the trade, live in the soil at different levels (depending on temperature and moisture, among other things). Subterranean termites search for food, which is cellulose (wood) and the (subs) build tubes to protect their fragile bodies from weather and enemies.

Your enemy is the worker subterranean termite. This is the little guy that does the damage. There are also soldier subterranean termites in the same tubes, wood damage, and nest, but they are the guards to fight off the enemies, hence, their mandibles. There are also one or more queens in the nest. These nests send out swarmers which try to mate and establish new colonies.

Not many of these "swarmers" get started as most die one way or another, but the ones that do start a colony lay about 400 eggs per hour so out of the thousands that start from

one nest, not too many have to survive.

To control subterranean termites
we try to take away their food by
removing all wood to soil contact and
by chemical treatment of the soil. In
controlling (subs) and before chemical
treatment, the protective tubs should
be broken down and scraped from
foundations and piers. Also remove
tubes from any wood members as these
are their highways to destroy your
structure. Termite tubes will be
found under heater pipes, sewer pipes,
around fireplaces and in connecting
patio, steps, porches, and throughout
the subarea.

Subterranean termites have been
found in the attic of homes and three
stories up in apartments, mostly under
the siding or stucco, but also up the
framing and fireplace. See Diagrams
A-1, A-2, A-3, A-4, B-2, B-3, F-1, F-
2.

A typical termite report will show
a foundation diagram of the property,
and locate the area of damage. These
are typical diagrams (S-1, S-2).

On a foundation diagram the letter
(S) usually means subterranean termites, (K) usually means drywood termites, (CD) means cellulose debris,
(F) stands for fungus (wood rot), (EM)
stands for excessive moisture, (FG)
usually means faulty grade, (Z) means
dampwood termite, (B) means beetles,

(SL) means shower leak. See Diagrams S-1, S-2.

All termite companies may not use this type of coding. Most companies have a code or number system they use to note areas of infestation or infection on termite reports.

As for repairs, some wood members only slightly damaged by subterranean termites can remain, if these wood members are still "structurally sound." This, in most cases, means 10% or less damage to the wood member. However, the building inspector has the final word, as he is the one who signs his name to the building permits and is the one who will have to answer if there is a problem later.

Some states or counties may require trenching on both sides of the foundation to chemically treat the soil 12 inches below the surface, then replace the soil.

This trenching is also used on all sides of piers and plumbing.

DO NOT TAKE CHANCES

USE SHARP TOOLS

PULL OR BEND OVER NAILS

DO NOT TALK TO SOMEONE WHO IS USING
A POWER TOOL

CHAPTER 8

CONCRETE STEPS, PORCHES AND PATIOS

On Diagrams S-2 the (S) at the step, the porch, and the garage are typical of subterranean termites entering the structure. Termites can enter via concrete steps and garage floor voids. These areas are not bonded to the foundation well and the smallest crack can let subterranean termites enter. Holes are normally drilled in the top of the slab, 6 inches apart and chemicals, such as Chlordane, Aldrin, Dieldrin or Heptachlor, are injected in the soil below the step, porch or garage floor.

As these chemicals are very hazardous, read the label and follow the manufacturer's directions carefully. A better way is to have a pest control company come and inject the chemical. They are licensed and insured. In fact, just disposals of the containers that the chemicals come in is a problem. Some states and counties may not allow chemical treatments. In areas such as these, the building inspection wants repairs made in ways to block entry of subterranean termites. Some of these ways include removing a strip of concrete at the infected area, installing metal flashing and re-pouring concrete with good bonding. Also, leaving space open to inspection. (See Diagram E-1)

Patios built against the structure sometimes cause easy entry of subterranean termites and fungus rot. When the patio is higher than the adjacent foundation, moisture can enter the structure, causing damage. (See Diagrams E-3, E-4) Wood strips in patio, butting against siding, brings subterranean termites and fungus rot to the structure, with good possibility of damage. (See Diagram E-2)

These wood strips that butt the siding should be cut off and replaced with concrete. When concrete patios, etc., are higher than the foundation, a concrete retaining wall should be installed. This is done by removing a strip of concrete from the patio, adjacent to the structure. (See Diagram E-4) Dig out soil to below top of the foundation and remove siding or stucco from bottom, to 12 inches above top of patio. Then install continuous metal flashing, passed both ends of the patio by 6 inches. Build a form and pour a continuous concrete retaining wall, sloped at the top, to divert moisture. Metal flashing should extend above retaining wall and under siding, when siding is replaced. (See Diagram E-4)

A good bond is important. In some areas the building inspector will want the metal flashing to be waterproof (use tar). I like to use duplex nails (double head) when I nail on the flashing. This leaves a head sticking out for the concrete to grab. Many other methods also work well, but remember, the easy way is often the best way. You don't want the retaining wall to pull away from the structure in years to come (hence, the duplex nails).

When ordering concrete mix for retaining walls, I would suggest you use pea gravel (small rocks in the mix). The space is small and this size gravel in the mix (concrete) will flow well. The pea gravel can also be used when filling in the area cut out of the patio.

Hand mixing the concrete for the retaining wall is recommended, as it usually takes less than a cubic yard and you don't want to pay for more than you can use. (One cubic yard is usually the minimum price.) The ready mix concrete companies have to charge standby time and filling the retaining wall form can be a slow job. (See Mixes and Seals)

Another advantage to mixing your own concrete for small pours, is getting the mix to the job site. It's much easier to transport (wheelbarrow) dry mix than wet concrete.

When the base of wooden stairs are damaged, see embedded wood members.

```
BE CAREFUL, WATCH YOUR STEP
```

```
USE THE RIGHT TOOL FOR THE JOB
```

```
DO NOT WORK ALONE, IT IS NOT SAFE
```

CHAPTER 9

DRYWOOD TERMITES

Drywood termites can be chemically treated, if you can get the chemical to them, and therein lies the problem. If the wood members are accessible often what is done is to drill holes in these wood members and inject chemical under pressure into the holes. Quite often while injecting the chemical, the chemical will squirt out one of the other holes. Then you know you have hit the channel eaten into the wood, and the chemical is reaching the drywood termite. Eye protection is essential for this type of work.

The type of chemical used for this work is the wood preservation penta-chlorophenol (penta).

It should be mentioned here that most times termite companies will recommend fumigation to kill drywood termites, which is the proven way. It is also very expensive for the property owner and very profitable for the termite company. However, at times, fumigation is the only way to get to the drywood termite, but I feel it's overdone because of the profit in fumigation.

These drywood termites can be in closed areas such as hollow walls, between subfloor and finished floor and in areas of the attic too difficult to reach. The drywood termite is also found in firewood and this has led to infestation of the structure. Stored firewood is always checked when found in the garage, house or adjacent to the structure.

Drywood termite infestation is generally found by their droppings, which is like coarse sand, light to darker tan in color, and barrel-shaped. Often some of these barrel-shaped droppings can be seen at the injection hole in the wood members (this is a good place to drill a hole) for injection of "penta" chemical.

It is rare to repair damage caused by the drywood termite, as they are slow eaters and do not seem to reproduce very fast. It seems to take a large infestation before they send out swarmers (the winged sexual termites) to start new infestations. Over the years, I have repaired hardwood floorings, paneling and some structural members. But most damage is from something else.

In the event you should repair some drywood termite damage, the drywood termite dropping should always be removed or covered over. Then, if there is an inspection of the area again (and there should be) the inspection will show if there is activity in the treated area. (There will be more droppings.) This is also true if the structure is fumigated.

Removing wood paneling from the wall is best done by driving the finish nails through the paneling with a nail set. (Thereby leaving only one small hole, which can be easy to fill.) Now it is possible to chemically treat the back of the paneling and kill the insect without damage to the paneling finish. Penta is brushed on the back of the paneling in a well ventilated area and allowed to dry before re-installing paneling. Always use chemicals in accordance with manufacturer's instructions. Check the framing if possible after the paneling is removed for infestation to the adjacent area.

If the framing adjacent to the area, where the paneling was removed, shows signs of infestation (small holes or droppings) or if you are not sure, I would recommend chemically treating the area. This is best done by the drilling of holes in the framing (1/4 inch or smaller) about 2/3 or 3/4 through the framing on a downward direction. Then pressure treat, by injecting penta chemical into the holes with a garden sprayer or an oil squirt gun. Care should be taken to protect household goods and carpeting from spills and sprays from back pressure from the holes. Eye and face protection should be used. Holes can be closed by use of wood dowels driven into the holes or filler to plug holes.

Furniture infested with drywood termites can be taken to a fumigation company. They usually have a room in which they fumigate furniture.

The fumigation company will also fumigate furniture infested with other types of insects.

CHAPTER 10

DAMPWOOD TERMITES

As the name implies, these termites live in damp wood. Dampwood termites are seldom chemically treated, as the controlling of the moisture is enough to kill them. If a termite inspection reveals dampwood termites, look for fungus (wood rot) to be present also. These termites are mostly found along coastal areas and fog bound areas. The wood must stay damp for these termites to survive.

Repair damage, correct moisture problem and chemically treat area of repairs with a fungicide, copper green or penta. Seal and paint if necessary.

WATCH OUT FOR THE OTHER GUY

WEAR GLOVES

GROUND ALL ELECTRIC TOOLS

CHAPTER 11

BEETLES

If the termite inspection indicates beetles, there are many types. One is old house borer. This is mostly found on the east coast of the United States and in Europe. Although this insect may do serious damage to structural wood members, chemical treatment is usually not called for as these insects need moist wood and soil to survive.

Keeping the wood members dry and painted will usually protect the wood from the old house borer. Air circulation over the soil is also important. Cover the subarea soil with plastic (polyethylene) to protect wood members from reinfestation, as this insect lays its eggs in the soil. Use a fungicide such as copper green or penta on areas of repair.

True powder post beetles mostly infect hardwood, false powder post beetles mostly infest soft wood and bamboo beetles mostly infest bamboo. Small infestation of these insects can

be treated with penta pentachlorophenol but large infestations will
probably require fumigation (see chapter on fumigation). Remove all droppings after repairs and fumigation,
re-inspect areas to make sure infestation is killed.

CHAPTER 12

PLANTER BOXES

Planters built on the soil against the structure should be checked carefully to see if they are sealed. Sealed means that the moisture cannot leak into the structure. This is accomplished by a watertight metal pan or the inside of the planter is sealed with tar. There are other ways also, but this is what is usually accepted as sealed. (See Diagram C-6)

Planter boxes attached to the framing or siding should also be sealed. (The metal pan is mostly used in this type planter box.) In most cases, removal is the cheapest and best way to correct the problem.

Planters built inside the structure can also cause damage and should also have a metal pan to control moisture.

TIE-OFF THE LADDER AT THE TOP

BE AWARE OF YOUR SURROUNDINGS

WHILE WORKING

CHAPTER 13

LEAKING STALL SHOWERS

To test for a leaking stall shower, you must seal the drain in the shower with a plug or tape. (I use masking tape.) Next fill the shower floor with 2 inches of water.

Then go under the shower and check for water leaks. If the shower is on the second or more floors, there will be stains on the ceiling. The water test should be for at least 15 minutes.

Most of the showers checked will be from under the house (subarea). Look for stains and fungus damage, and wood stains to the floor and supporting wood members. There will probably be a wet spot or a dent in the soil, where the water has been hitting the soil.

Many ways have been tried to stop the leaks, some of which are to re-grout the tile at the floor and two rows of tile from the bottom. Also to paint the floor with "Thompson's Water

Seal." I don't know if these work and if they do work, I don't know how long these "corrections" would last. However, with the high cost of shower repair, most of us have to look for a cheaper way.

To repair the stall shower that is leaking at the floor, you must first get the building permit from the building department, then remove the shower floor and two rows of tile from the bottom up. Remove the inside and top of the dam, which is the raised area under the door. When it is a corner stall shower, with glass walls, remove the inside of the dam under the glass wall also. This is so a water-proof membrane can be re-installed between the wood and the masonry. If the floor is a concrete slab and re-pair is needed, because of a leaking floor, a membrane is still needed. (See Diagrams F-3, F-4, F-5, F-9, F-10)

To remove the shower floor it is best to use a 2 or 3 pound hammer, a cold chisel and a lot of work.

Remove the tile, repair the wood floors and any structural wood members, then chemically treat the area of repairs with a fungicide.

Call the building inspector out to OK your work. Then if OK you can call a tile setter. He will have a pan installed. The pan must be filled with water and the building inspector must OK the pan as being watertight. I think it is better to have a pan man do the pans, as they guarantee their work, to the point that if the pan leaks in a year they will have the shower repaired free. They can do that messy job cheaper than I could. After the pan is inspected and signed off, the tile man will finish the job, or you can try it yourself. If you plan to do it yourself, pick up some how to information when you buy your tile and grout. Check into it, it's easier than you think.

An even cheaper and I think better way to do the job is to install a metal, plastic or precast shower pan. This installs on top of the wood floor (no pan man needed). Then bring the wall tile down to the pan. You may have to lower the shower door to meet the new pan.

However, if you plan to go with a metal, plastic, or precast pan, you may have to install a new floor covering also. I think the saving you make by going to preformed pan will more than likely pay for a new floor covering. These preformed pans only come in limited sizes, which are usually standard sizes. There is an additional bonus and that is these preformed pans seldom leak if installed and cared for properly.

DO NOT USE WATER AROUND ELECTRIC

CORDS OR TOOLS

KEEP CHILDREN AWAY FROM WORK AREA

CHAPTER 14

RAISING THE FOUNDATION

First get a building permit. Raising a building's foundation is easily done by first, supporting the area adjacent to the raise (see Diagram C-3) by installing shoring to take the weight off the foundation where work is to be performed.

Nail a straightedge board on area framing. (See Diagram C-1) Then cut framing studs by setting an electric circular saw on top of straightedge board and cut off damaged wood members in a straight line. Next remove all wood members below cut. Remove only small area at a time (about 6 feet on one story buildings and less on two or more stories). Install mudsill as shown in Diagram C-2. Drill holes in mudsill for foundation bolts and jack bolts (see Diagram C-4). Place at least 2 jack bolts into holes and force mudsill up to the studs and insert foundation bolts. Redwood or cedar is recommended for mudsills. Install flashing to separate framing from concrete. (See Diagram C2) Then install reinforcing steel and tie it to the foundation bolt bottoms, where it will be in the concrete pour.

A jack bolt is a piece of all-thread with a nut and a washer. I like to use 3/4 inch all-thread or larger. Some termite workers use pieces of pipe and drive them in with a hammer, but I feel the jack bolt does a better job.

If more foundation must be raised on this wall, you just repeat the steps just performed. However, use caution and only raise one side at a time. Don't make too long a raise on one wall as you could loose the whole building, if you are not careful.

Next, build the inside forms and brace them well (but not to the shoring). See C-5 for one way.

After the building inspector has signed off the form, meaning you can pour the concrete, build the outside forms and brace well. (See C-5) To make the pour easier, sometimes you can install a chute and pour the concrete from outside. Outside pours is much easier. If you can't pour from outside, then with the help of another person, the concrete will have to be fed under the structure. Then a person under the structure will fill the form with concrete.

Make the concrete mix so it will run well (but not too loose). To pour the concrete from under the house, you must get the concrete to the person under the structure. If there is a vent that is close, it can be removed and the concrete fed to the subarea and into the "sled." See how to build sled in Chapter 23. Then the form can be filled. I wear rubber gloves for this, as I find it is easier to get the concrete into the tight areas with my hands rather than a coffee can, which many termite workers use. Some companies use concrete pumps for big pours, to make the job go faster and to save on man-hours. However, they are expensive to rent. Tap on the form to remove air as you pour concrete.

After the concrete is poured and the mess cleaned (tools washed and cleaned, etc.), you are through until the next day, when you can remove the forms and see how the pour came out. Sometimes there will be honeycomb, or rock pockets in some of the pour. These can be easily filled with dry pack (see Mixes and Seals). These honeycombs or rock pockets are caused by air locked in under the concrete (a bubble). An easy way to remove most of them is to tap on the form with a hammer. Tap (or beat) with the hammer on the wood next to the concrete, not the bracing.

In some cases you will be able to use cinder blocks (building blocks made from sand and cement). However, these should not be used (in my opinion) when there is a moisture problem.

The cinder blocks are joined together with mortar (see Mixes and Seals) and moisture penetrates these joints fairly easy.

Foundation bolts will have to be placed where they will fall into the holes in the cinder blocks.

No form or bracing is needed. Remember to fill the holes in the cinder blocks and if possible use some reinforcing steel to tie the blocks together (if more than one row of cinder blocks). Steel goes between the blocks horizontally. In the holes vertically.

Sometimes the foundation raise is only a matter of inches (up to 6"). In this case, quite often what is done is to dry pack (see Mixes and Seals) a new foundation under a wall or post, etc. Dry pack is used in construction jobs quite a bit. To raise a foundation with dry pack, cut off the damage and install a new mudsill. The mudsill should have bolts or nails sticking out of the bottom as this will grip the dry pack. The existing concrete should also have nails or bolts sticking out to grip the dry pack.

With a board or form braced on one side, you can dry pack from the other side. This is done with a hammer or the end of a 2x4 or anything that will force the dry pack into the opening and pack it tight. Then let the dry pack set for about a half hour. Then finish it using a trowel to cut away the extra dry pack (see Diagrams C-7, C-8).

It should be noted here that dry pack is not as strong as concrete and should be used accordingly.

It's the rocks in concrete that gives concrete its strength along with the cement and sand. Also the dryer the concrete is mixed (while still being wet), the stronger (generally) the concrete will be. So don't add too much water, only enough to make it workable.

ON BIG JOBS, RENT A TRASH CONTAINER

WATCH FOR WIRES

CHAPTER 15

FAULTY GRADE

A faulty grade exists when the soil is above the foundation. This can be corrected by lowering the soil. (See B-3) However, at times the soil under the structure is too close to the wood framing that supports the floor. This is a major job and requires removing the soil from under the structure to a safe level. I don't know of any easy way to do this, it's just a hard job that must be done.

If the faulty grade is just to a pier post (or one area), the soil can be moved and spread out to correct the grade. (See Diagram S-2)

When the structure has a concrete floor with a bathtub on this floor, there is a plumbing hookup near the drain end of the tub (where the plumbing goes under the concrete floor from the tub). At times this area is a faulty grade also. This is easy to correct by simply removing the soil to a safe level. The tub access area sometimes has subterranean termites and fungus damage (wood rot). (See Fungus Damage chapter)

RENT LARGE TOOLS

CHAPTER 16

EMBEDDED WOOD MEMBERS

Many times door jambs are embedded in the concrete floor, steps or other areas. These wood jambs collect moisture and become fungus infected or damaged by termites. These should be cut off above the damage and dry packed (see Mixes and Seals, and Diagrams D-1, D-2, D-3).

Posts are also embedded in patios and damaged from moisture and termites. Support posts under stairs and in basements have also found to be damaged.

These posts are usually cut off and footed with a concrete base, which means to drive large nails into the cut end of the post and dry pack a masonry base onto the post.

The nailing of 2 pieces of wood to the base of the post will help hold the dry pack in while you get the post set. Sometimes a hole should be drilled into the concrete floor under the post and metal bar or nails inserted to hold to the dry pack. Make sure the post is plumb.

Wood steps that are fungus damaged or are embedded should be supported and then a concrete base step (cbs) installed. (See E-5) To install a concrete base step, the stringer (side of steps) must be cut off to the right height (standard steps are 7"-7¼"). A form for concrete is built and braced to the height of the cut-off stringer bottom. (See Diagram E-5) Install large 16p nails into the stringer to concrete base steps. Chemically treat wood members. Call for building inspector to OK the work. Then pour the concrete. After concrete is poured, tap with a hammer on outside of form to remove air pockets from wet concrete. Level off and finish the top of the concrete step. When the concrete is starting to take a set, at this time, it is possible to brush the top with a broom to give the step a non-slip finish. Edge the step with edging tool to round off the corners of concrete step. (See Tools)

CHAPTER 17

ATTICS

Attics are at times inaccessible for inspection due to insulation, storage, etc. At times there is no access to the attic, in the case of a flat roof.

The areas of the attic that can be inspected may show infestation of drywood termites or beetles. The termite company may recommend fumigation, and indeed fumigation may be the best solution to the problem. (See B-5) However, if the infestation is local (a small area), the infestation can be chemically treated with penta (pentachlorophenol). This is done by drilling holes in the infected wood members (don't drill hole all the way through the wood members), and then pressure treat. Use a pump type oil can to inject the chemical in the holes.

If droppings (from the insect) are found above the ceiling, look for small holes in the wood member directly above the droppings. Drill and treat this area.

Protect the ceiling area from drips and spills as this chemical will penetrate through the ceiling and show an oil spot on the painted surface of the living area. A plastic drop cloth is usually used. Make sure the chemical will not eat through the plastic.

At times fungus (wood rot) damage is found in the attic. This should be cut out and removed. Chemically treat the area of repairs, after repairs are made. Protect the ceiling from drips and stains with plastic. Attic areas should be dry and well ventilated.

At times the vents are blocked. This can lead to fungus damage. Correct vent problem where it exists. Insulation sometimes blocks vents between the rafters. These vents between the rafters must be open to allow flow of air for removal of moisture.

Care should be taken in working or moving in the attic. One false step and there will be a hole in the ceiling. Only walk and stand on the joist.

CHAPTER 18

FUNGUS DAMAGE (WOOD ROT)

Fungus damage (wood rot) will be found in many places. Wood windows and doors are prime areas for fungus (rot) if not maintained properly. These windows and doors should be sealed from moisture, both inside and outside. Moisture from condensation on the inside glass will run down to the wood members and start the fungus (rot).

Paint or varnish seal well, but if damage is present repair first. Minor repairs can be made with Spackle, or a floor repair compound. If used outside the filler should be waterproof when dry and then painted. If the damage is major, then replacement is usually the best way to go. There are shops in most towns and many in cities that do millwork. Some lumber companies carry wood windows of different sizes, or they can order the size you need. The door can also be ordered from lumber companies.

Wood thresholds and windowsills

are also prime areas of fungus damage. Thresholds get a lot of traffic over and on them at the doorway. So I would recommend replacing them. If possible use metal as it seals better and is cheaper than hardwood thresholds.

Windowsills that are heavily damaged with fungus (rot) should be replaced or repaired. Sometimes the damaged wood can be cut out and new wood replaced. After the repairs and painting, it's hard to tell there was ever any damage. Windowsill stock can also be found at the lumber stores.

Wood trim and wood siding are also damaged by fungus (rot). The amount of damage determines the replacement of the wood member or the removal of the rot and filling with a filler. In either case the repaired area should be chemically treated with a fungicide.

Handrails and wood decks that are butting the structure, and are damaged by fungus (rot) or subterranean termites, can be separated from the structure with metal flashing. This means to install metal flashing between the infected or infested wood members and the structure.

Also, wood fences that are attached to the structure (wood siding or stucco) should be separated with metal flashing, as this is easy access for subterranean termites and fungus (rot). (See B-4)

The theory is that any wood that is attached to the structure and also in contact with the soil (no matter how remote) is an easy access for fungus (rot) and subterranean termites to enter the structure. Often I have seen this (theory to be true when tracing down the origin of the infestation or infection). It is important to find where the infection or infestation started, in order to chemically treat the area, or stop the reason for the damage (such as a leak). If the origin of the damage is not found, the repairs will soon be damaged, and maybe more.

Fungus rot is found under brick and masonry stairs and porches. Many times the masonry is built over a wood frame and the wood is separated from the masonry with a waterproof membrane. When this membrane leaks, there is no protection for the wood members and fungus (rot) is the result. In this case, it is best to remove the damaged wood members and resupport with pressure treated wood that is protected from moisture with plastic or some other waterproof material. Chemically treat all areas of repairs and get building inspector to sign repairs off. It is best to seal the stairs and porch as best you can to keep moisture out. Seal from the top with latex caulk, or some other sealer (see Mixes and Seals).

Eaves and roof overhangs often are damaged by fungus (rot). (See chapter on Excessive Moisture) When wood stays wet or damp for any length of time, fungus (rot) starts to grow.

WEAR PROTECTIVE CLOTHING

CHAPTER 19

STUCCO REPAIRS

Minor stucco repairs are easy to do. However, matching the existing finish is sometimes hard to achieve. I have found that a sponge trowel or a paintbrush dipped in water helps to get best results.

If structural repairs are to be made, the building department should be notified and work signed off by the building inspector. The building inspector will also want to inspect the lath (chicken wire), keep it tight.

Stucco is made of at least two coats of stucco. They are the scratch coat and the finish coat. The scratch coat can be built out to about one quarter of an inch (1/4") of the finish level (see G-1). When the scratch coat is set (but not dry), the soft cement coating is scratched (making grooves in the cement) with a scratch tool (or a screwdriver if small area). On larger areas, lawn rakes have been used. This scratch is important as a base, and the grooves in the scratch will allow the finish coat to grip the base coat. Allow scratch coat to dry 10-14 days before applying finish coat. Allow finish coat to dry 10-14 days before painting. (See Mixes and Seals)

Vents are installed in stucco buildings as shown on Diagrams G-2 and G-3. To install a vent, break away stucco 4 inches larger than the vent to be installed. Cut and bend stucco wire (lath) out of the way. Cut out wood members as needed. Drilling of large holes will help get a saw started. Be careful of wires and pipes. Repair or replace building paper (felt paper). Nail on the vent. Be sure to have the right side out as some vents can be used for wood siding also (see Diagrams G-2, G-3). Call the building department, the inspector may want to check framing. If checked and ready for the next step, install lath wire (stucco wire) using furring nails. (This will allow stucco to get under the wire.) See Diagrams G-3, G-4. Bring old ends of existing wire down over the top of the new wire. Nail down all the loose ends. I find a small nail like a 4p is about right for this. When the lath (stucco) wire is complete, it will have to be inspected by the building inspector. Now you are ready for the stucco scratch coat. (See Mixes and Seals) I usually mix stucco in the "sled" or a plastic bucket. The plastic bucket is easy to clean, even if the mix dries. All you have to do is hit the sides and the dry mix falls out. Make the mix with just enough water to make the mix creamy. Using a metal trowel and a "Hawk," fill the void with stucco mix. Don't worry about getting the stucco even as that can be done before the stucco dries. Use a spoon trowel to get (in) next to the old stucco. Let stucco set. Then when the stucco is ready (not dry), scrape off the excess stucco 1/4 inch below finish (old) stucco, use a straightedge to judge distance. Close is good enough in the scratch coat. Now scratch the scratch coat and let it dry. See Diagram G-1. When the stucco scratch coat has cured (dried) for about 10-14 days, you can apply the finish coat, or have a plasterer do it, if you don't think you can match the existing texture.

Doing the finish coat is about the same as doing the scratch coat. You put the stucco on the same way. Then, using a wood float or a rubber sponge float, you level off the new stucco finish to match the existing stucco. Then with the wet rubber sponge trowel or a wet brush (paintbrush or whisk broom), you can feather out the new stucco finish and try to match the original texture. Let finish coat dry 10-14 days before painting.

Stucco arches and fences as shown in Diagrams B-2, B-4 are sometimes made of wood framing. This wood frame can become damaged by fungus (wood

rot) and subterranean termites. If
the stucco fence is connected to the
structure, the infestation and infection can be transferred to the building.

To correct this, the best way I
have found, is to remove the wood
member at the area adjacent to the
building, and pour a concrete plug.
See B-2 for the same procedure used on
archway.

Check with building department, as
they must OK all repairs. The remainder of the fence or arch can also be
gutted (remove all wood, etc.) from
the top (leaving the finished outside
stucco). The stucco shell will have
to be braced before filling with concrete. Light weight concrete is
available and may be best if used in
archway.

CHAPTER 20

FUMIGATION

Fumigation must be performed by a company licensed to do such work. This is a hazardous and expensive job. All living things should be removed prior to the start of the job. The building will have to be under fumigation for 12 to 24 hours, in order to get a kill. This is usually determined by placing a live termite in a hole in a block of wood and a plug in the hole. When the gas penetrates the wood and kills the termite, it is assumed that the other termites or beetles are also killed.

I always remove, or cover over, the droppings of the insect where I can. If these droppings are not removed or covered over, the next time the building is inspected, another fumigation will be called for, even if there is no live infestation. The fumigation company guarantees the kill for usually a year, and will refumigate if an infestation reoccurs. However, the way a termite inspector finds drywood termites or beetles is

to look for the droppings, so cover
the droppings, then you will know.

Plants should be heavily watered
just before the fumigation and right
after and maybe they will survive.
The vines growing on the house usually
die back, but may survive also.

CHAPTER 21

CHEMICALS

All chemicals should be used in a safe manner, following manufacturer's instructions carefully.

Chlordane can be purchased by homeowners. This chemical is mixed with water to a 1.0% emulsion. This mixture is then used as a soil poison to block subterranean termites at the soil. To apply chemical under the structure, use hose attachment or liquid chemical pump. Application should be 1 gallon of mixed chemical to every 10 feet of crawl space (sub-area under house). Heavier chemical treatment should be applied to foundation area at a rate of 4 gallons of mixed chemicals per lineal foot. This 4 gallon rate of chemical treatment should also be applied to plumbing and pier blocks (intermediate supports). (See Tools)

Most large hardware stores sell the chemical Chlordane, for about $50.00 per 1/2 gallon. One-half gallon is usually enough for the average home.

The chemicals Aldrin, Chlorpyrifos, Dieldrin, Heptachlor, Isofenphos, and Lindane, must be purchased and used by certified pesticide applicators.

I recommend having a termite company or a pest control company apply the chemicals. These chemicals are very hazardous and one should protect himself from the chemical when using, and keep them secure when not in use. Lock them in a safe area.

Wood preservatives are also toxic and should be used as manufacturer directs.

Penta (Pentachlorophenol) and Copper Green (copper Napthate) are the two most used wood preservatives. These wood preservatives can be purchased at most hardware stores.

All chemicals should be stored in a safe locked place.

CHAPTER 22

TOOLS

Most tools used in termite work are carpenter tools, concrete, cement finishing tools and some plumbing tools. Of course, if linoleum is to be laid or ceramic tile installed, there are special tools used for this.

One of the first things needed is protective clothing, such as coveralls, gloves, hat, kneepads, dust mask, and work shoes.

Handy tools include all carpenter type hand tools, hammer, level, saws, tape measure, knife, etc.

Power tools can be rented, such as electric saws, drills and rotohammers. Power activated tools which shoot a nail into concrete or steel are also rented, as are pumps and concrete finishing tools. Droplights and extension cords are inexpensive to purchase.

A chemical applicator, that attaches to a garden hose, is useful if a liquid chemical pump is not available. (See "Build Your Own")

Ladders are something every household needs. There are linoleum cutters which can be purchased to cut round holes in soft tile or linoleum, then drill into concrete floor and replace plug.

Reciprocal saws (where the blade goes in and out) is a tool much used in termite repair. This tool takes many types of blades to cut wood and metal. This tool can also be rented.

CHAPTER 23

BUILD YOUR OWN

Sled: Cut two pieces of 2x6 three (3) feet long and half round each end. On the rounded end (which will be the bottom), nail on a piece of flat tin. (See Diagram T-1) Now attach a rope, if you like and this sled will help move tools, concrete, cellulose debris, bricks, etc., in the subarea. The sled is also useful for mixing small batches of concrete or stucco. I usually place the sled below the area I am stuccoing and the stucco droppings fall into the sled for reuse. The sled can be made any size you like, however, this size worked well for me. (T-1)

Liquid chemical pump: This is simply a pump of any kind, that will build enough pressure to push the liquid out of a garden hose. I used an old washing machine motor and a pump that I bought at the local hardware store. Both the motor shaft and the pump shaft should be the same size. Then buy a connector and connect the motor and pump. With different fittings you can make garden hose fit any pump (see Diagram T-2). Then with a pistol grip type sprayer nozzle, you can spray or send a stream of chemical to reach across the subarea.

You also will need a barrel for the mixed chemical, 50 gallons is what I use. The pump and motor can be attached to a board or to a hand truck. I have found many uses for the pump other than termite work.

Be careful not to use the hoses used for chemical work, to drink from, or wash with, there may be chemical residue left in the hose.

The pick-up hose that goes in the barrel can be purchased at the hardware store also. I use the short remnant hoses. When spraying the subarea always start furthest from the access and work your way out. You don't want to crawl through the chemical you just sprayed. A mask should also be worn for spraying.

Trenching may be required. (See page 29)

CHAPTER 24

MIXES AND SEALS

Concrete: Ready mix concrete delivered in mixer trucks is best. To mix small batch, mix 1 part cement, 2 parts sand, 4 parts gravel or 1 cement to 6 concrete mix. Use type 1 cement or sacked concrete mix and clean water.

Stucco: 50% sand 50% cement mix with water to creamy mixture, use for scratch and finish coats. Use sack mortar mix or sacked stucco mix, purchased at building supply stores. Use to plug holes drilled in concrete. (Insert cardboard in hole to hold mix.)

Dry pack: 50% sand 50% cement, mix half of mix with water to creamy mixture, then add other half. Mixture should look like dry ball of sand. Sacked mortar mix can also be used. To match color of concrete pour use sand from concrete mix.

Mortar mix: 40% sand 10% lime or fire clay and 50% cement, mixed with water to stiffen mixture, so it will stand up like whipping cream. Best to use sack mix.

Plug holes in concrete, use stucco or mortar mix on top of paper plug inserted in hole.

Pour-a-rack: Fast drying cement mixture for patch jobs. Purchase at building supply stores and hardware stores.

Floor filler: Mix with water and use in 20 minutes as it sets fast and hard in a short time. Use this to make thin repairs to floors. This also repairs other wood damage. (Purchase at building supply, paint, linoleum, and hardware stores.)

Can Spackle: Wood and Sheetrock filler.

Dry Spackle: Mix with water, use same as above.

Taping compound: Use for Sheetrock joints and filler.

Grout: For ceramic tile (can be colored).

Caulking compounds: Some caulks and some uses:

Butyl-Flex: enclosures and masonry
    stairs
Tub and tile: use on shower, tub
    enclosures

Latex: Use on shower, tub enclosures and linoleum
Polyseamseal: Seal masonry stairs and enclosures
Silicone: Enclosures, masonry stairs.
Rubber: Enclosures, masonry stairs.

KEEP RENTED TOOLS IN USE OR

RETURN THEM

PROTECT THE PUBLIC FROM CHEMICAL

STORE ALL CHEMICAL IN LOCKED AREA

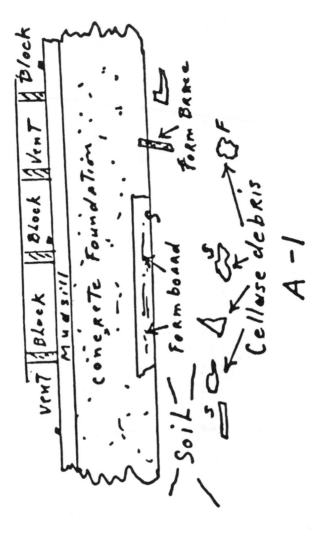

Block · Vent · Block · Block · Vent · Block

Mudsill

Concrete Foundation

Form board

Form board

Form Brace

Soil

Cellulose debris

A-1

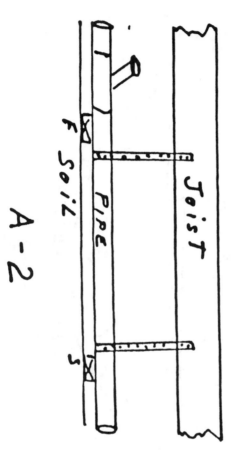

A-2

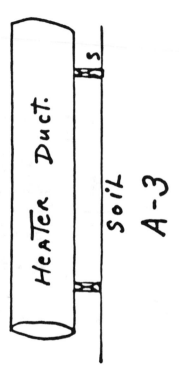

Heater Duct.

Soil A-3

Heat
Unit

S

Soil

A-4

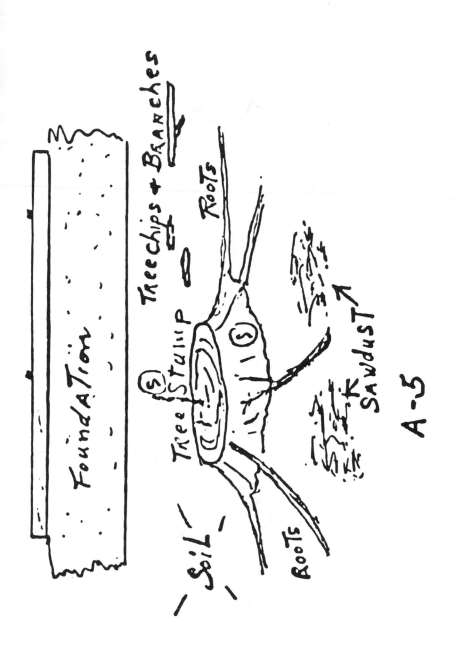

A-5

85

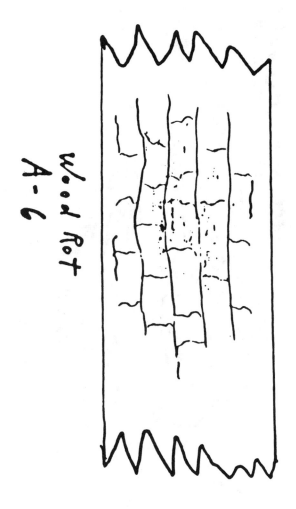

Wood Rot
A-6

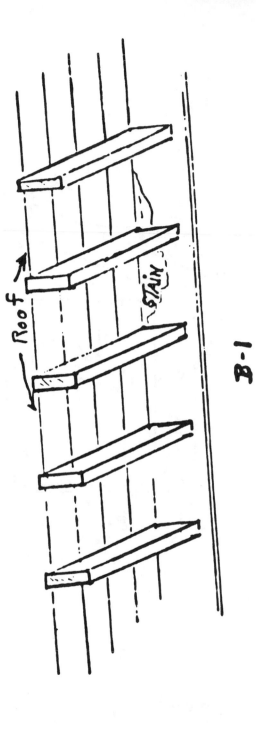

over hange or eve

Roof

STAIN

B-1

87

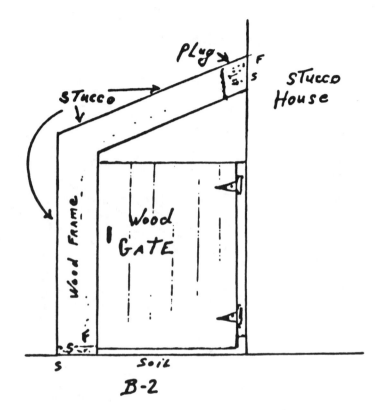

Plug

Stucco

Stucco House

F
S

Wood Frame

Wood GATE

F
S

S

Soil

B-2

Concrete Slab   Beam Cieling

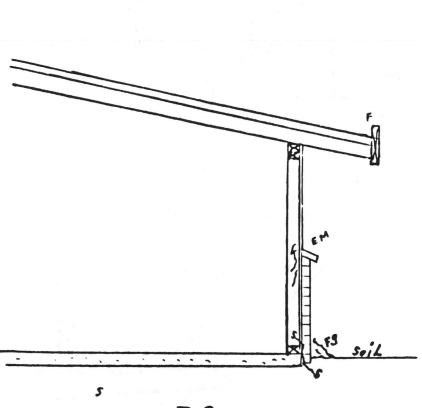

F

EM

FS

soil

S

B-3

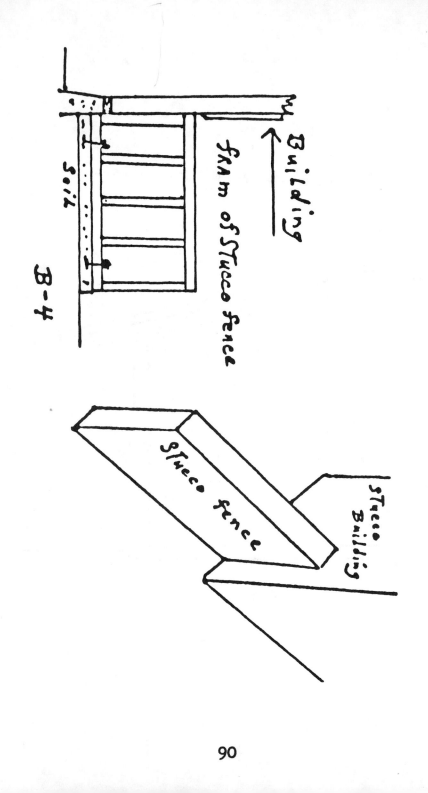

Building

Fram of Stucco fence

Soil

B-4

Stucco fence

Stucco Building

90

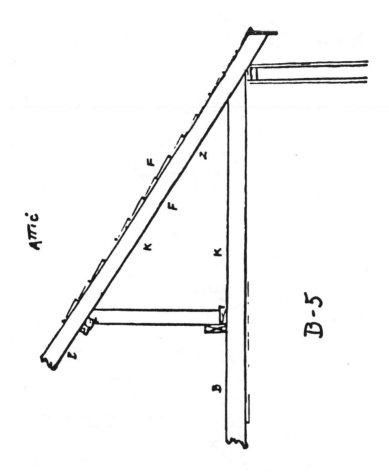

Attic

F

F

Z

K

K

L

B

B-5

91

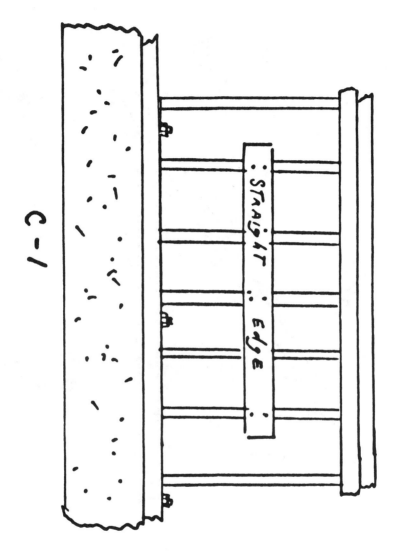

C-1

STRAIGHT EDGE

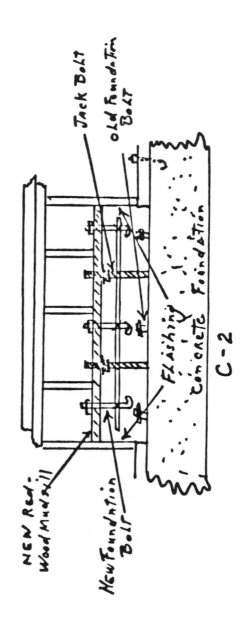

Jack Bolt

old Foundation Bolt

Flashing

Concrete Foundation

NEW Redw. Wood Mudsill

New Foundation Bolt

C-2

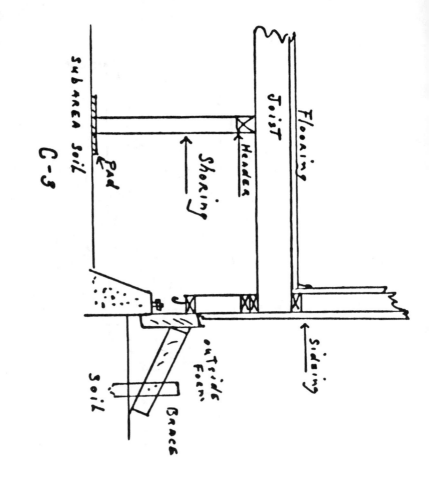

C-3

Subarea soil

Flooring

Joist

Header

Shoring

Pad

Siding

outside form

Brace

soil

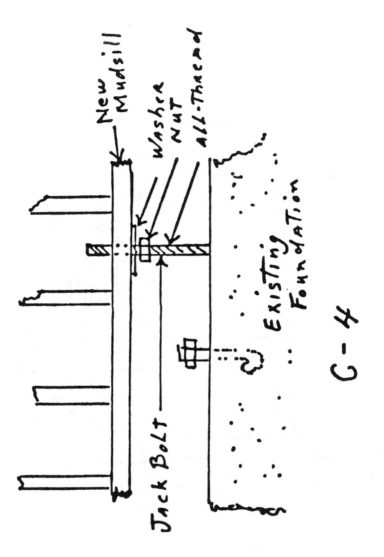

New Mudsill

Washer
Nut
All-Thread

Existing Foundation

Jack Bolt

C-4

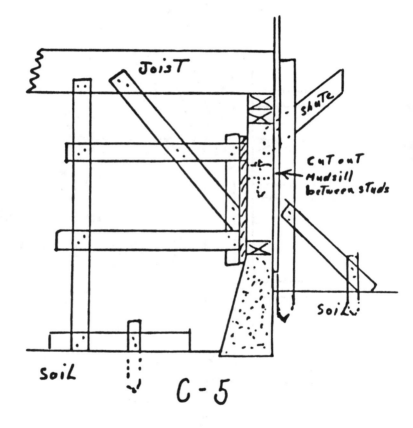

JoisT

shuTe

CuTouT
Mudsill
beTween sTuds

Soil

Soil

C - 5

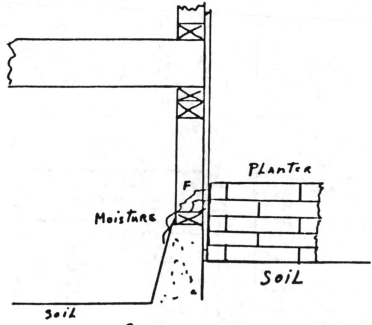

PLANTER

Moisture

F

SOIL

soil

C-6

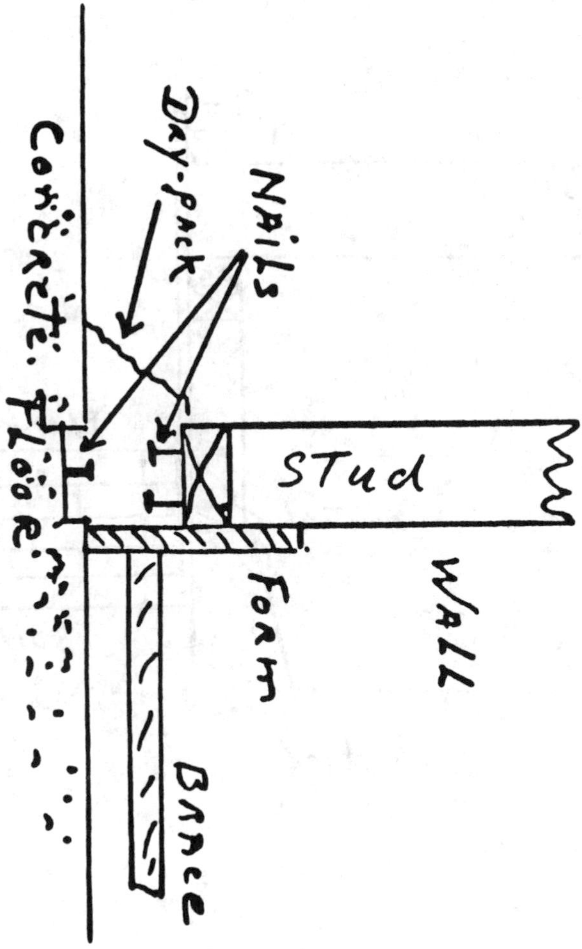

C-7

Nails

Dry-pack

Concrete Floor

Stud

Foam

Brace

Wall

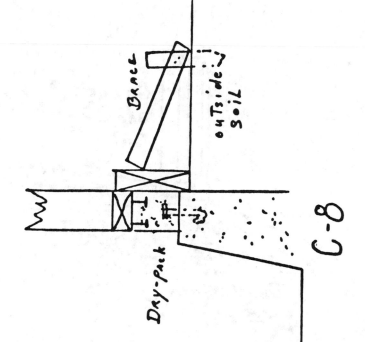

Brace

Dry-Pack

ouTside Soil

C-8

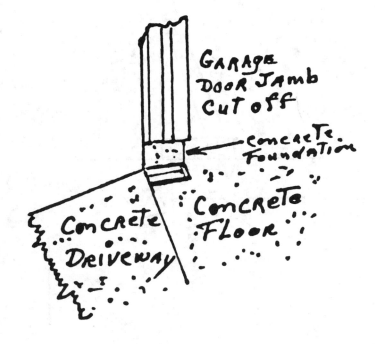

GARAGE
DOOR JAMB
CUT OFF

← Concrete Foundation

Concrete Floor

Concrete Driveway

D-1

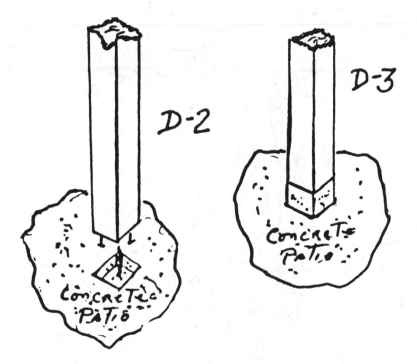

D-2

D-3

Concrete Patio

Concrete Patio

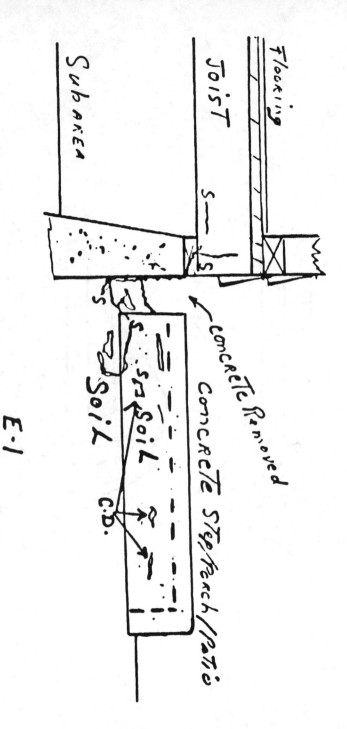

E-1

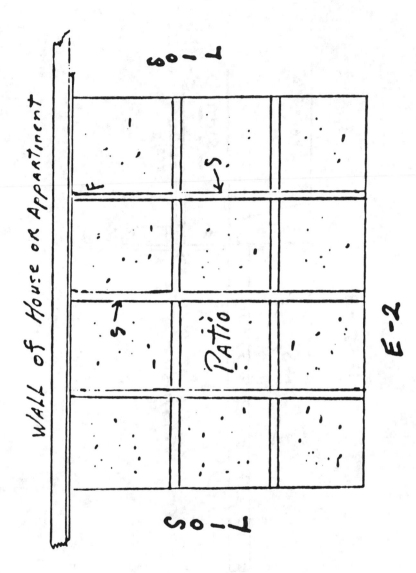

WALL of House or Appartment

T-os

T-os

Patio

S

S

F

E-2

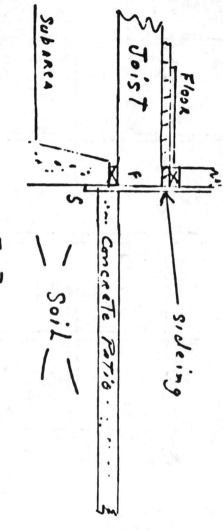

Subarea

Joist

Floor

siding

S

Concrete Patio

E-3

Soil

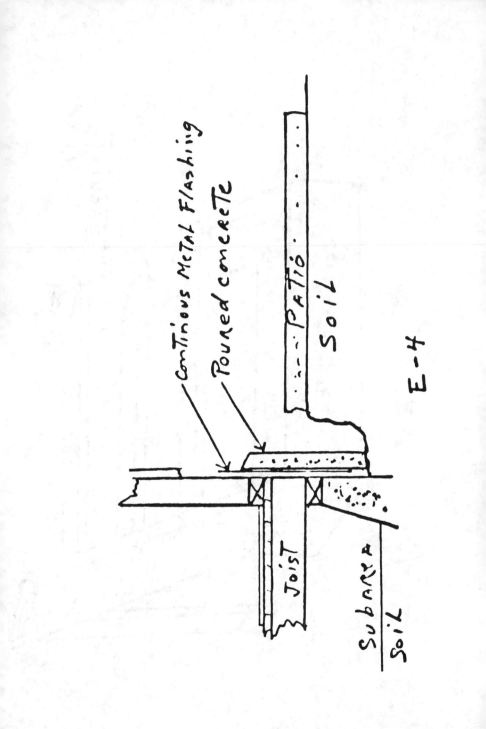

Continous Metal Flashing

Poured concrete

PATIO

Soil

Joist

Subarea Soil

E-4

105

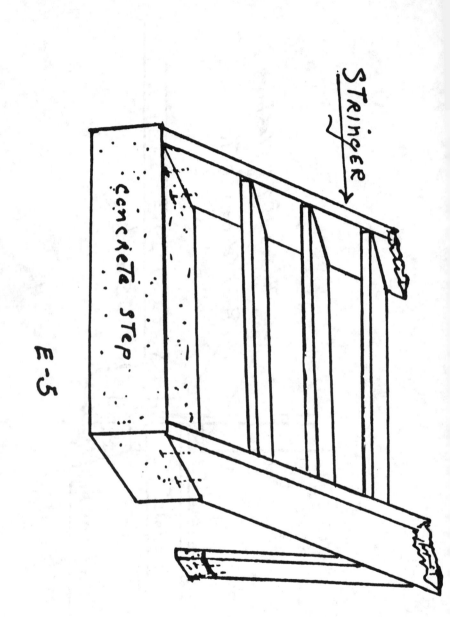

STRINGER

CONCRETE STEP

E-5

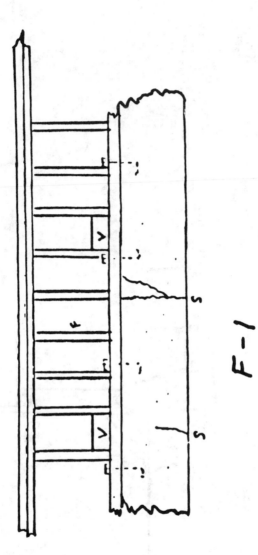

F-1

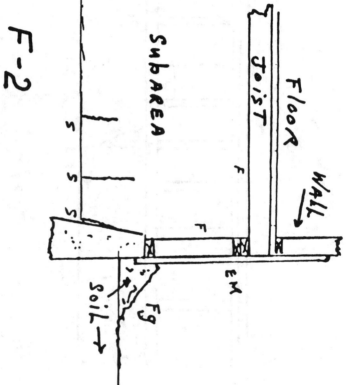

F-2

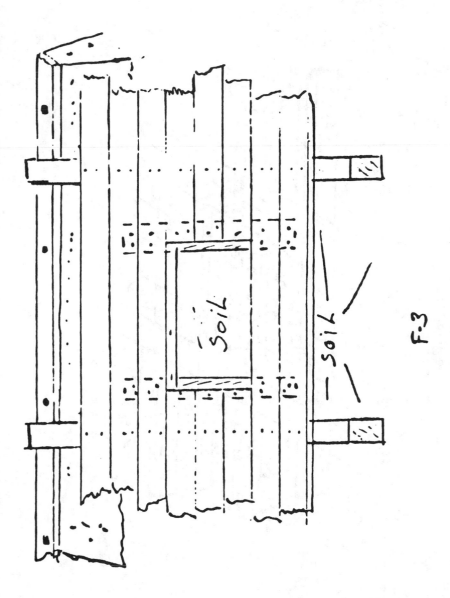

soil

soil

F-3

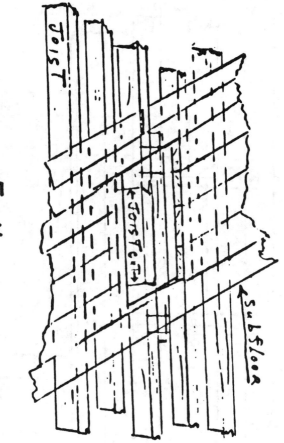

F-4

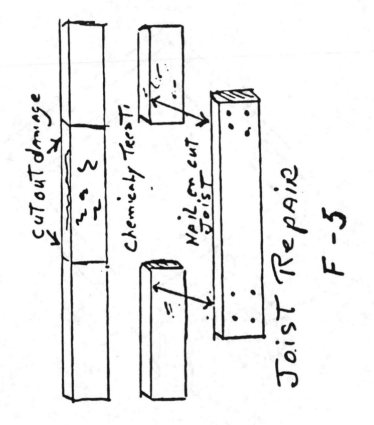

cut out damage

Chemically Treat Ti

Nail in cut Joist

Joist Repair

F-5

111

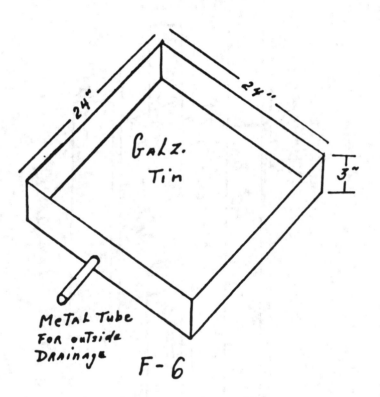

24"

24"

Galz.
Tin

3"

MeTaL Tube
For outside
Drainage

F-6

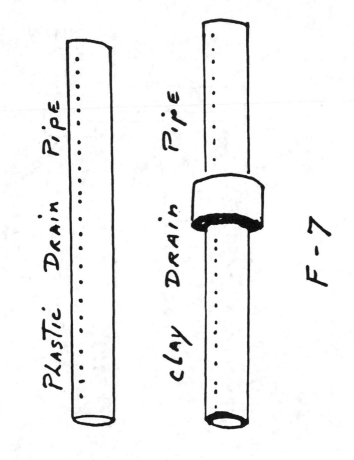

PLASTIC DRAIN PIPE

CLAY DRAIN PIPE

F-7

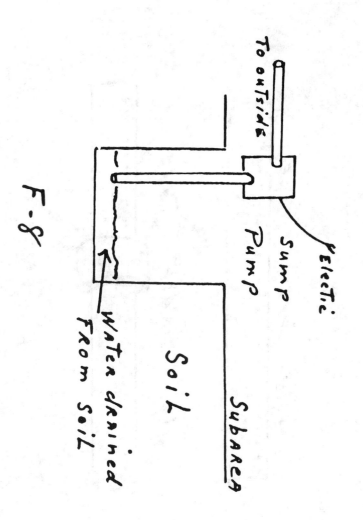

To outside

Electric

Sump
Pump

Water drained
From Soil

Soil

Subarea

F-8

114

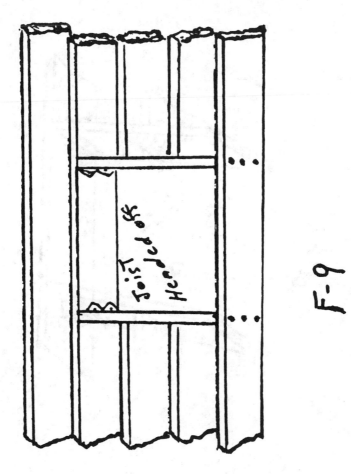

Joist Headed off

F-9

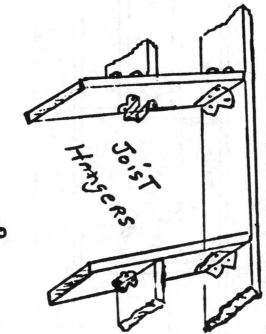

Joist Hangers

F.10

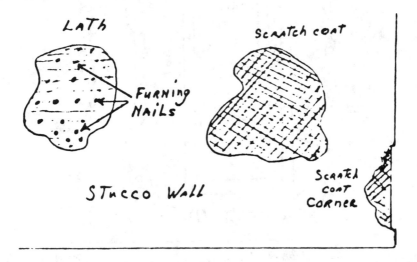

Lath

Scratch coat

Furning Nails

Stucco Wall

Scratch coat Corner

G-1

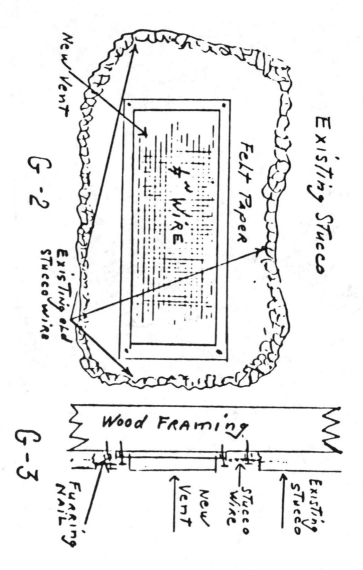

Existing Stucco

New Vent

Felt Paper

4" Wire

Existing old Stucco wire

G-2

Wood FRAMING

G-3

Funring Nail

New Vent

Stucco wire

Existing Stucco

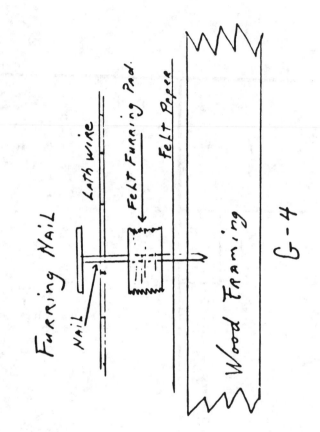

Furring Nail

Nail

Lath wire

Felt Furring Pad.

Felt Paper

Wood Framing

G-4

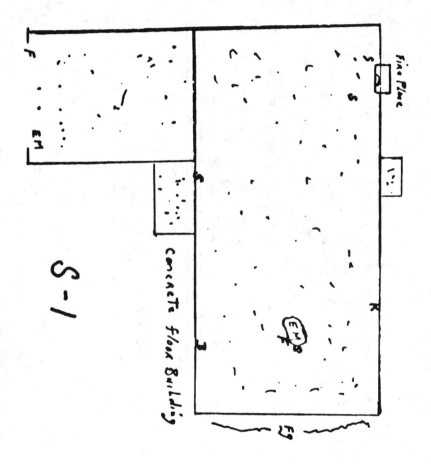

S-1

Fire Place

Concrete Floor Building

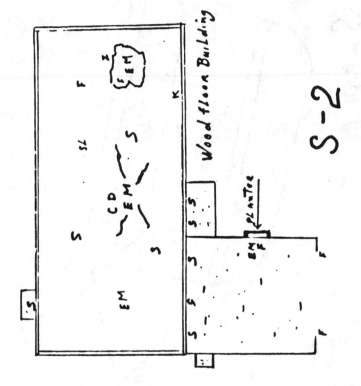

Wood Floor Building

S-2

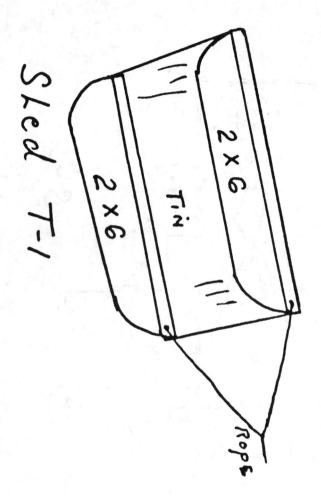

Sled T-1

2×6

2×6

Tin

Rope

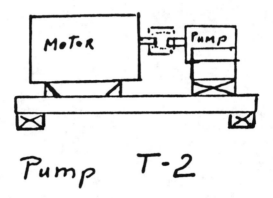

Pump T-2

NOTES

CHECK-OFF LIST FOR HAND TOOLS

Wood saw

Hammer

Nail puller

Hacksaw

Single jack (3# hammer)

Calk line

Level

Tape measure

Wrench (12 inch)

Chisels

Keyhole saw

Flat-bar

Whisk broom

Metal cement trowel

Wood float trowel

Putty knife

CHECK-OFF LIST FOR HAND TOOLS

Tapping knife

Paint brush

Pliers

Nail set

Rags or paper towels

Funnel

Dust pan

Ladder

Rope

Broom

Sheet metal shears

Wire cutters

Bucket (plastic)

Brick trowel

Eye protection

Dust mask

CHECK-OFF LIST FOR HAND TOOLS

Roll of plastic sheeting

Screwdriver

Garden spray can

Oil squirt can

Kneepads

Sheetrock knife

Staple gun

Cardboard box

Coveralls

Bump hat

Brad pusher

Linoleum knife

Spoon, cement trowel

Edging, cement trowel

Sponge (big)

Linoleum roller

CHECK-OFF LIST FOR MATERIAL

Redwood

1x4	2x4
1x6	2x6
1x8	2x8
etc.	etc.

Structural wood

1x4	2x4
1x6	2x6
1x8	2x8
etc.	etc.

Plywood

½   ¼

Particle board (underlayment)

½   ¼

Trim wood
    door jambs
    window parts
    stucco molding

Sheetrock
    nails   tape   mud

Foundation bolts

Jack bolts (nuts & washers)

Nails

common	finish
4d	4d
6d	6d
8d	
16d	

Stucco
    wire   paper   nails